GOD'S
LESSON PLAN
for EDUCATORS

A WEEKLY DEVOTIONAL TO HELP YOU
GET THROUGH THE SCHOOL YEAR

CHARLIE 'CJ' BUTLER

CONTENTS

DEDICATION

This Devotional is dedicated to every educator that feels lost along the way. This is not an easy profession. However God has called you to it and he will equip you for it. I also thank my wife, Janelle, for being my inspiration to become an educator. It was one of the best decisions that I have made. To every student that I have and will come in contact with, thanks for making me better. Thank you Dallas and Charlee (my children) you are my inspirations to keep Going!

GET STARTED

Isaiah 43:18-19

18 Remember ye not the former things, neither consider the things of old.

19 Behold, I will do a new thing; now it shall spring forth; shall ye not know it? I will even make a way in the wilderness, and rivers in the desert.

Ready or Not, the new school year is here! It seems as if the summer has just flown by, and now, we are back at work. Take a deep breath! It's going to be ok. God is going to use *you* this year. *You* have been called to this! We all know that being an educator is more than just a profession; it's a calling. It's not for the money and fame, or the lack of it, but it's for the fulfillment we get from seeing young lives changed. God has strategically placed students in your classrooms or the workloads you have this year just for you. Each of these people and situations need something different, and *you* are equipped to meet their needs. The past is the past! Don't bring old mindsets and past issues into your new year. The prophet Isaiah tells us that God is doing a new thing (Isaiah 43:18). *Anything that God does is a Great thing.* Therefore, we are getting ready to walk into a new and Great year. It states that "*he will make a way in the wilderness and rivers in the desert*" (Isaiah 43:19) God is about to make sure that you have all that you need this year and that you are able to go through any obstacle or test that may come your way. What seemed impossible last year, will be possible this year with God. Jesus told his disciples in Matthew 19:26 that "With man this is impossible, but with God all things are possible." Have faith this year that all things are possible, even the hard things. Start this new year off by declaring this will be the *Best School Year* that I have ever experienced! You must believe "that eyes have not seen, ears have not heard, nor has it entered the hearts of men all the things that God has in store for you" (1 Corinthians 2:9). In order to get to the end of the year, you have to start the year! Start the Year with Faith, and End it with Victory!

FEEL JOY!

Philippians 4:4

Rejoice in the Lord always. I will say it again: Rejoice!

Start this school year, start this month, start this week, and start this day feeling Joy!

Joy is a feeling of great triumph and happiness. My prayer for you is that you feel joy this week. As we start this new school year, you are probably experiencing a lot of differing emotions. However, I want Joy to be the strongest one you feel. Find Joy in everything you do this week. Even if something crazy happens, speak to it and say, "Something Good Has to Come out of This!" Make it Your business to Feel Joy This Week.

Prayer Starter:

Father In the Name of Jesus, help me control my feelings today and this week. I will experience a lot of new things and meet some new interesting people. Help me feel joy this week. Help me experience the Joy that you give. Help me realize the power of having Joy. And so I take authority over my emotions and have faith that Joy will overflow me this week. Thank you, God, for the precious gift of Joy. I will rejoice every day this week because you have blessed me with Joy. Thank you for Joy.

In Jesus's Name,
Amen

LIVE IN PEACE

2 Corinthians 13:11
Finally, brothers and sisters, rejoice! Strive for full restoration, encourage one another, be of one mind, live in peace. And the God of love and peace will be with you.

When you first think of a classroom or school, peaceful is not a word you would use to describe them. However, even in the midst of chaos and confusion, you can live in peace. Take up residence in peace. Change your address to peace. Let peace be the place where you rest and spend the majority of your time. Take peace with you wherever you go. Think of peace like an American Express card you can't leave home without. As you are packing your things to leave home to come to school make sure that you pack your peace, because you will need it to make it through the day.

This Week's Agenda:

What are areas in your life that you need peace in?
What are the steps that you are going to take to obtain that peace?

BE JOYFUL

Romans 12:12
Be joyful in hope, patient in affliction, faithful in prayer.

Who am I going to be this week? As educators, we have to be a lot of things to a lot of different people. It may feel like each day you have to put on a million different costumes. However, this week I want you to be joyful. Be joyful in hope, that means you will rejoice in the hope that this will be a great week for you. Also be patient in the affliction and trouble that may come, just know that God is working it out in your favor. Being patient is defined as being able to accept or tolerate delays, problems, or suffering without becoming annoyed or anxious. This week, things that used to bother you at school won't bother you. God also wants us to be faithful in prayer this week. Prayer is your main mode of communication with God. Keep the lines open and talk to him all day and every day he will aid you in making it through this week. Just be joyful this week. That's all God wants for you is to be joyful.

Philippians 4:6-7
6 Be anxious for nothing, but in everything by prayer and supplication, with thanksgiving, let your requests be made known to God; **7** and the peace of God, which surpasses all understanding, will guard your hearts and minds through Christ Jesus.

This Week's Agenda:
Be Joyful, Be Patient, Be Faithful

A SAFE PLACE

Psalm 46:1-3

1 God is our refuge and strength,
an ever-present help in trouble.
2 Therefore we will not fear, though the earth give way
and the mountains fall into the heart of the sea,
3 though its waters roar and foam
and the mountains quake with their surging.

In all of our classrooms and different areas of the school, there are posted evacuation maps. They tell us where to go if something happens such as a natural disaster, or a fire, there are designated areas to go to to keep us safe from harm. As educators, we also have a safe place where we can go, and that safe place is God. He is our help, our safe place, and our evacuation shelter. Protector and helper are a part of who he is so when you are feeling lost this week, go to him in trouble, and go to him when you're feeling down. Go to him, he is our help. He is our place to go. Don't fear, have faith in our help which is God. So as the scripture says God is our refuge and our strength, therefore I don't have to be afraid.

This Week's Agenda:

Find your Place of Refuge in your school!

FILL ME UP

Romans 15:13
May the God of hope fill you with all joy and peace as you trust in him, so that you may overflow with hope by the power of the Holy Spirit.

We are in week five and I am sure you have experienced a lot in the short amount of time: tests, lesson plans, observations, lectures, parent, teacher, conferences, lunch duty, discipline problems, and the list goes on. At this point, some of us are feeling drained and empty. You are pouring out so much of yourself, but not being refilled. My prayer for you today is that you allow God to fill you up, and let him fill you with joy and peace. Trust him to give you just what you need to keep going. Don't throw in the towel just yet you just need a refill. As you are reading this God is overflowing you with hope, joy, and peace. The windows of heaven are open and you are standing under an open portal ready to fill you up. Joy, hope, and peace are coming to you right now! Feel them as you are being filled. Can you feel the power in these feelings?

Prayer Starter:
Father God, thank you for the Joy you are giving me right now. I was feeling empty but now I am filled with your joy and Your joy is my strength. Thank you for opening up the windows just for me and I am standing in a posture ready to be filled. So my cry today is Fill me up Lord, till I overflow.
In Jesus Name
AMEN!

MAKE PEACE

1 Peter 3:11
They must turn from evil and do good;
they must seek peace and pursue it.

Listen, I know there have been plenty of opportunities in the last five weeks for you to act up. I mean act up badly, but I am so proud that you didn't. You have been tested and you have passed the test. I know you have given a test to your student but you have passed the test. The enemy is on his job to disturb your peace and he will use anything or anybody to do it. However, we have power over him. You have power over him so this week pursue peace, be the peacemaker and the calm to the storm in your classroom or office this week. Do good and don't let anyone make you do or be evil. Matthew 5:9 states "Blessed are the peacemakers, for they will be called children of God." Let's be good children of God this week by pursuing and making peace.

This Week's Agenda:
Put the devil under your feet this week. Memorize this scripture and demonstrate your power:

Luke 10:19
I have given you authority to trample on snakes and scorpions and to overcome all the power of the enemy; nothing will harm you.

GOD'S PLAN

Jeremiah 29:11
For I know the plans I have for you," declares the Lord, "plans to prosper you and not to harm you, plans to give you hope and a future.

Nothing is worse than something throwing a monkey wrench in your well-thought-out lesson plans for the week. Your time was well spent planning out your instruction, meetings, and tasks for the week, and here comes something to mess it all up. It can really mess up your entire mood or vibe for the week. I have a question for you, what did God have planned for you this week? Do we consult him in our plans for the week, have you asked God what he wants for you this school week? Have you asked God to show you the way to a successful week? Let's start including him in the planning process. Basically, we just need to follow His plan for our lives. He will make things easier if we just follow God, his plans always work so scratch what you had planned and go to God in prayer. Let him lead you and watch how great this week will be. Simple instructions-follow his plans.

This Week's Agenda:

Pray for your week and listen to God's instructions and STICK TO HIS PLAN!

SING YOUR SONG

Exodus 15:2
"The Lord is my strength and my defense;
he has become my salvation.
He is my God, and I will praise him,
my father's God, and I will exalt him.

There are many songs you hear your student singing, rapping, or listening to in their loud AirPods. Most of the songs we don't know, some of them we do know, some we may like, and some of them we don't like. My question for you today in week eight is what is your song? What is it that you sing to make it through the school day? The scripture above tells us that the lord is your song, he is the reason why you sing, so sing a song today. Singing brings joy and happiness. It's an expression of love and thanks to our God, so this week show God how much you love and appreciate Him by singing your song. You may not be the best singer, but you still have a song. Praise Him today, Praise Him this week, and it will make you feel better. Sing a Song and have a great week.

This Week's Agenda:
Find your Song or Write your Song and SING IT!

Psalm 104:33
I will sing to the LORD all my life; I will sing praise to my God as long as I live.

CHANGE THE WAY YOU THINK!

Acts 26:2

I think myself happy, King Agrippa, because today I shall answer for myself before you concerning all the things of which I am accused by the Jews,

I am sure that numerous thoughts have gone through your mind as we come to the close of this first quarter. You are putting grades in and getting ready for report cards. You may have to schedule conferences for students who are behind, and you probably have a holiday coming up while you will be at school in-service. I know what you were thinking but let's change it. I encourage you to think yourself as happy. You have power over your thoughts. Philippians 2:5 teaches us that we must have the same mindset or attitude as Jesus. I hear you, you say I am not Jesus. That is a true fact, but we are striving to be more like him. Let's start by changing the way we think this week, good vibes only this week. Good thoughts only this week, positive thinking only this week if you change the way you think you can change the way you live.

This Week's Homework:

Think on these things:

Whatsoever things are true, whatsoever things are honest, whatsoever things are just, whatsoever things are pure, whatsoever things are lovely, whatsoever things are of good report, if there be any virtue and if there be any praise (Philippians 4:8)

DON'T FAIL!

John 16:24

Until now you have not asked for anything in my name. Ask and you will receive, and your joy will be complete.

Until now, you have been trying to do this by yourself. Until now you have thought you were strong enough to handle this on your own. This is a tough job. This is not an easy profession and like me, I know you feel you don't need another professional development. We need the Lord's help. Whatever you need from him. All you have to do is ask big or small, just ask him. It's just like one of your students who's failing your class because they refuse to ask for help. Don't fail this thing we call life because you fail to ask for help. Like the hymn says, ask the Savior to help you. He is willing and able, he will carry you through. Go ahead and ask for what you need from God. Matthew 7:7-8 "Ask and it will be given to you; seek and you will find; knock and the door will be opened to you. **8** For everyone who asks receives; the one who seeks finds; and to the one who knocks, the door will be opened." So this week we are asking, seeking, and knocking. So much is about to OPEN up in your life. Ask for It and Get Ready to Receive it.

Today's Agenda Item:

Write out the things you're asking God for this week:

1. _____

2. _____

3. _____

4. _____

5. _____

I AM OK!

Philippians 4:6-7

Do not be anxious about anything, but in every situation, by prayer and petition, with thanksgiving, present your requests to God. **7** And the peace of God, which transcends all understanding, will guard your hearts and your minds in Christ Jesus.

There are probably a lot of things in your school that you don't understand. You don't understand why that meeting wasn't an email. You don't understand how you're going to implement all of this new stuff that they have come up with and still teach your standards. You don't understand why these kids won't turn in their work. You don't understand why the next holiday is so far away. There's a lot you don't understand but you are OK! Say it to yourself, I am 0K! Keep repeating it until you believe it. The reason why you were OK it's because you have peace. God has given us a piece through Jesus Christ that transcends all understanding. Let Peace guard your heart and mind and remember you are OK.

This Week's Agenda:

There is Power in your tongue!

Proverbs 18:21

Death and life are in the power of the tongue: and they that love it shall eat the fruit thereof.

So Declare it yourself this week, "I AM OK!"

COMPLETE THE WORK!

Romans 15:4

For everything that was written in the past was written to teach us, so that through the endurance taught in the Scriptures and the encouragement they provide we might have hope.

As an educator, you have a great amount of knowledge on different things. You also have some experience in the area that you are teaching. You have read a lot of books, watched quite a few videos, and sat through numerous PDs. All of these experiences have helped to shape you into the educator you are today. Your experience in life has helped you become who you are. Everything that you have gone through has been a learning experience. I pray it has brought you closer to God. God has a record that is second to none. You should be encouraged to have the hope that he can and we'll do anything. With God, All things are possible so anything that comes in your way is not too hard for God. He can handle it, and He will handle it. I've got a secret for you. He's already working on it. Be encouraged today because God is on your side.

This Week's Agenda:

Be encouraged that the work that God has started in you will be completed.

Philippians 1:6

And I am certain that God, who began the good work within you, will continue his work until it is finally finished on the day when Christ Jesus returns.

GIVE ME STRENGTH!

Psalm 119:28
My soul is weary with sorrow;
strengthen me according to your word.

Thirteen weeks probably seem like and feel like it has been longer than it really is, life has truly been "lifeing!" However, you are still here and regardless of how rough it's been you have made it and I don't believe God has brought you this far to leave you God knows exactly what you are going through and exactly what you need. You need strength! My prayer today is that the Lord will strengthen you. I'm glad you are reading this devotional because it's strengthening you, I'm glad you're praying because it is giving you strength. I'm glad you are reading your word because it is giving you strength. You will succeed, and you will endure because God is strengthening you right now.

This Week's Agenda:
Your prayer every day this week is "Lord give me strength!"
Watch God make you stronger each day.

THE RIGHT DIRECTION

Psalm 16:11
You make known to me the path of life;
you will fill me with joy in your presence,
with eternal pleasures at your right hand.

Do you ever send a student somewhere with a pass and they never get there? You are pretty sure they know how to get to the office or the media center. However, somewhere along the way they go off the path. Sometimes they get lost or take a detour just like the students we get off the path. However, we must always get back on track. Whose path are you following, yours or someone else's, or God's plan? I hope you are choosing God's path because it's the right path. Proverbs 14:12 There is a path before each person that seems right, but it ends in death.

In the above text, Psalm 16:11 we are instructed that on God's path, we will be filled with joy and eternal pleasure. That sounds like a path I would like to be on and follow, follow God and he will lead you to where you need to be.

Prayer focus for the Week:
Your prayer this week should be just to ask God to lead you in the right direction and your response should be to go where He leads me. I will follow, and I'll go with him all the way.

GOOD SLEEP!

Psalm 4:8
In peace I will lie down and sleep,
for you alone, Lord,
make me dwell in safety.

There have been many times when students have gone to sleep in my class. My first thought is dang my lesson can't be this boring and then I begin to realize that there are many reasons why that student may be sleeping in my class. Obviously, they needed some rest. Rest is something we all need and don't usually get as educators. We need rest to help rejuvenate our bodies from the taxing day at school. However, there are many reasons why we don't get rest. My prayer is that we overcome all of those reasons and allow God to help us rest this week and the weeks ahead. In peace as the text says you will lie down and sleep. It's hard for me to sleep in a place where I don't feel safe. God is giving you a spirit of security so you can rest and feel safe in his presence so you can get the sleep and rest that you need to continue.

This Week's Agenda:

Make this declaration, "I will rest this week. I will have a good night's rest tonight and every day this week I will continue, and I will win this race."

BLESS ME, LORD!

Psalm 147:11
the Lord delights in those who fear him,
who put their hope in his unfailing love.

If there is one thing a teacher needs from their students it's respect. Without it, it's hard to get anything accomplished in class. As a respected teacher, you can pull stuff out of students that others can't, so it's very beneficial for you to have the respect of your students. God also wants our respect. We should honor and reverence him; he delights or takes pleasure in it. When we respect and honor Him he floods us with His unfailing love. There is nothing that he will withhold from us. Let's show God some respect this week and then begin to receive his love. No educator wants to see a disrespectful child come into their classroom. So when God looks at you what type of child does he see? We are all His children, but we choose to be one of the respectful ones.

This Week's Agenda:
Honor God this week and watch what he Blesses you with.

Psalm 84:11
For the LORD God is our sun and our shield. He gives us grace and glory. The LORD will withhold no good thing from those who do what is right.

WHO CAN I RUN TO?

Proverbs 18:10
The name of the Lord is a fortified tower;
the righteous run to it and are safe.

I strive to make sure that my classroom is a safe space. I want all of my students to feel safe to learn and be themselves, I work very hard at this. However, when reading this scripture I ask myself where is the safe place for the educator who is making us feel safe to be ourselves and teach, and I couldn't come up with an answer. We must create our own safe space, and Jesus is the center of that place, he is the one that keeps us safe. I know there is a separation of church and state but there are times of my day. I have to call on the name of Jesus. So feel safe to call on the name of Jesus. Find some believers in the building and create a safe place for you to worship and get encouragement throughout the day.

This Week's Agenda:
There is power in the name of Jesus and you should be able to call it wherever and whenever you want. Use His name for your safety! So this week your task is to create your very own safe place in your school.

FIND THE JOY!

Nehemiah 8:10
Nehemiah said, "Go and enjoy choice food and sweet drinks, and send some to those who have nothing prepared. This day is holy to our Lord. Do not grieve, for the joy of the Lord is your strength.

We have made it to the end of the second quarter and the first semester. Hallelujah, you are either about to go on Christmas break or have just finished. It is time to celebrate the goodness of God, celebrate every victory you have had this semester small or large. Guess what, you were still here! You may be bruised, tired, and ready to give it up but you made it this far. This is a time to renew ourselves and get strength for the second half. Give yourself a good pep talk and finish this year strong. The joy of the Lord is your strength. Be happy and be strong, find joy in every situation, make yourself laugh, and enjoy work in life. I know this is easier said than done, but give it a good try. What's the saying? Nothing beats a failure but a try. Try, try, and try again! You're not in this alone God is on your side but you've made it this far.

This Week's Agenda:

What are your Plans for the second half of the year? Make sure you include Joy in the Plan!

I HAVE PEACE!

2 Thessalonians 3:16
Now may the Lord of peace himself give you peace at all times and in every way. The Lord be with all of you.

It's time to begin the second semester and the countdown is on. We are just over the hump of the school year even though we are close to the end, there is still a lot to be done. I've got good news for you. You can do it. You have made it this far, just do it to the end. Paul gives us a boost this morning in this text when he says God will give us peace at all times and everywhere. That's some good peace, all the time and everywhere. You're about to become Peace. People will see you and recognize your peace all through the day. You will have peace everywhere you go! It's a promise and it's a gift, receive it today. He also reminds us that the Lord is with us. That's a great assurance to have at this point in the year, the Lord is with me!

This Week's Agenda:

Make the declaration today "I have peace because I know the Lord is with me." Take peace with you wherever you go and share peace around your school this week!

I'M EXPECTING GREAT THINGS!

Proverbs 23:18
There is surely a future hope for you,
and your hope will not be cut off.

What are you hoping for this week? Hope is a feeling of expectation and desire for a certain thing to happen. I pray that you expect great things for yourself this week. Great things will happen in your classroom this week because you expect it and believe God for it is going to happen expect nothing less than great things this week, look forward to it. The scripture states that your hope will not be cut off. That means nothing will get in the way of your greatness this week. As you read this, get ready for the great. 1 Corinthians 2:9 tells us that eyes have not seen ears have not heard, nor has it entered into the heart of man the things God has prepared for them that love him so if you love him, expect great things.

This Week's Agenda:

Make a list of the Great things that you are EXPECTING God to do for you this week:

Great Things List

_____

_____

_____

_____

FROM WEAK TO STRONG!

2 Corinthians 12:9-10

But he said to me, "My grace is sufficient for you, for my power is made perfect in weakness." Therefore I will boast all the more gladly about my weaknesses, so that Christ's power may rest on me. **10** That is why, for Christ's sake, I delight in weaknesses, in insults, in hardships, in persecutions, in difficulties. For when I am weak, then I am strong.

Are you feeling weak this week? Do you have the strength to endure? You may answer no to both of these questions however, I know someone who can help your weakness and give you strength. You should already know who it is. Yeah, you're right, it's Jesus. Through Christ, we receive the grace which is the remedy for our weakness. It's enough to carry us through weakness, is not something to be wary of because You have to be weak before you are strong. Life helps us keep strong, our experiences make us stronger. Don't be ashamed of your weakness. Give them to Christ so that you can receive his power. He gives me his power for my weakness. Sounds like a good deal to me, you will start the week weak but you will finish strong.

This Week's Agenda:

You don't have to be strong to be strong. God is strong enough for you. Your task is to rest in Him and allow Him to be your strength.

CHANGE OF CLOTHES

Psalm 30:11
You turned my wailing into dancing;
you removed my sackcloth and clothed me with joy,

I have a daughter in elementary school and at one point we sent her to school with a change of clothes just in case she had an accident. If something occurred and her clothes were messed up, she would have something to change into. We all have accidents, problems, and situations that mess our life up. Those things sometimes bring on bad feelings and emotions. However, the scripture tells us that God has given us a change of clothes. He knows that life is hard and he gets his own but because he is gracious, he lets us know that we don't have to stay. That way he takes your sad clothes and gives you happy clothes. He removes your grief and gives you joy. Change your clothes today and put on the items that God has laid out for you and you will change your week.

This Week's Agenda:

Every morning before you leave your house make sure that you have the right clothes on. Leave behind your clothes that will hinder your success this week. Only put on things that will lead to victory.

LET PEACE RULE

Colossians 3:15
Let the peace of Christ rule in your hearts, since as members of one body you were called to peace. And be thankful.

I know in this current time in America, police are not everyone's favorite, however, in history, police were referred to as peacekeepers. It was their job to keep the peace in the area that they were assigned. Oftentimes in our classrooms, we feel like peacekeepers and police. There are so many variables that we have to maintain and control. It can be overwhelming because all we want to do is teach, however, I present a different mindset to you today. Let peace keep you. Not just any peace, the peace of Christ, let it rule your heart today. The inner peace you experience will change your environment because regardless of what's going on, you will still have peace. Relinquish your control and let peace have its way with you this week!

This Week's Agenda

Let peace guide your decisions and conversations today. Make the decision today that you will not allow anything to disturb your peace.
Make this declaration, "I am a peacekeeper because peace is keeping me."

CONDITIONING

Isaiah 40:31
but those who hope in the Lord will renew their strength.
They will soar on wings like eagles; they will run and not grow weary,
they will walk and not be faint.

Many of us come into contact with many student-athletes within our school. Some of you may be former athletes. Most athletes have to go through what is called conditioning. Conditioning is defined as bringing something into a desired state of use. These athletes go through conditioning in order to prepare to compete during the season of their sport. Different types of training come into play to make sure they are prepared but as teachers, when is our conditioning? I've learned that I can't depend on anyone else to prepare me. That's my responsibility so I asked the Lord to help me prepare for this task. You may say it is the middle of the year but conditioning is still good because you will face a lot more stuff before the end of the year. Therefore put your faith and hope in the Lord he will renew your strength. You are getting your strength back; strong enough to endure and finish well. You will survive and you will succeed in every test. You can conquer and you will be able to run through every obstacle, walk through the rest of this year and not lose Hope because you are conditioned to win.

This Week's Agenda:
Read the story of Joseph in Genesis 37, 39-45.

THE RIGHT OUTFIT!

Ephesians 6:10-11
Finally, be strong in the Lord and in his mighty power. 11 Put on the full armor of God, so that you can take your stand against the devil's schemes.

One of the ways that a school gives an incentive to a teacher and a staff member is to let them wear jeans on Friday in exchange for doing something. They know some educators look forward to that day because they find jeans more comfortable. Most schools have a dress code that we must adhere to, so most of us have to think about what we will wear to work today. We want comfort, but we also want to be within the dress code. However, when we pick out our clothes, is the full armor of God in our outfit? We need and must have it on a daily basis. This scripture states that it will help us stand against the devil's schemes. We know we fight against a lot and we need the armor on, so you have to make sure that the full armor of God is in your wardrobe. You have to make sure that in your closet you have the helmet of salvation, the breastplate of righteousness, the shield of faith, the sword of peace, the belt of truth, and the shoes of peace. You have to make sure that you have all of that before you leave the house. It is just as good as the American Express card.

This Week's Agenda
You can never leave home without the armor of God. So make sure this week and every day from this day forward, that you leave the house with the right clothes on.

HE LOVES ME

Zephaniah 3:17
The Lord your God is with you,
the Mighty Warrior who saves.
He will take great delight in you;
in his love he will no longer rebuke you,
but will rejoice over you with singing

God Loves You! He loves you a lot. This is something that we need to be reminded of. He loves you so much that he will fight for you. His love causes him to look out for us and make sure we are protected. I know it's hard for some of us to feel loved by others so we have to be reminded that God loves us. He is our God, we are connected to Him and can take ownership of Him. Not only is He our God, but He is also with us. You may feel lonely at times, but always remember that God is with us. God takes delight in you, meaning he is happy that you are with him. This week rests on the fact that God loves YOU! What a Blessed Assurance!

Yes, He Loves Me Because the Bible tells Me So and He Demonstrates HIS love to ME!

This Week's Agenda:
Study Psalm 23 and realize just how much the Lord Loves YOU!

ACCESS

Romans 5:1-2
Therefore, since we have been justified through faith, we have peace with God through our Lord Jesus Christ, 2 through whom we have gained access by faith into this grace in which we now stand.

The key that I have for my classroom opens up a few doors around my school. However, the key admin has opened every door as an administrator. They need access to everything because of their position and responsibilities. There are times I need to get indoors, but I have to find an administrator to let me in because I don't have access. I feel like I should have access to these places, but I don't because of my position. I've got good news, through God, we have access to everything that we need by faith. We have access because I believe! I have access and nothing is off-limits concerning God. There is a whole kingdom out there, go for what you want. Your access has been granted this week. Walk into whatever God has for you. Nothing will block you because you have access.

This Week's Agenda:
Study and commit this scripture to memory:

Romans 8:38-39
38 And I am convinced that nothing can ever separate us from God's love. Neither death nor life, neither angels nor demons,[b] neither our fears for today nor our worries about tomorrow—not even the powers of hell can separate us from God's love. 39 No power in the sky above or the earth below—indeed, nothing in all creation will ever be able to separate us from the love of God that is revealed in Christ Jesus our Lord.

IT'S NOT IN VAIN!

1 Timothy 4:10
That is why we labor and strive, because we have put our hope in the living God, who is the Savior of all people, and especially of those who believe.

One of my favorite groups is The Clark Sisters, and they have a song entitled "My living in vain". In the song they ask the question if all of the things that they do are in vain, the questions are then answered with a resounding NO. It states that up the road is eternal gain. Basically, it means that God will reward us for all of our works here on earth. I know many of us to believe the things we do as educators are in vain. I want to let you know that your labor is not in vain. The students are paying attention whether they act like it or not. They appreciate you whether they say thank you or not. Keep doing the good work. There is a reward: You are needed and You are valued. We must keep striving and laboring in our Vineyard until our work is done. Be encouraged! God sees your work and payday is coming soon.

This Week's Agenda:

Believe the answer to this question, "Is my teaching in vain? No!"

Galatians 6:7-9
7 Be not deceived; God is not mocked: for whatsoever a man soweth, that shall he also reap. 8 For he that soweth to his flesh shall of the flesh reap corruption; but he that soweth to the Spirit shall of the Spirit reap life everlasting. 9 And let us not be weary in well doing: for in due season we shall reap if we faint not.

I CAN DO IT!

Philippians 4:13
I can do all this through him who gives me strength.

I must confess I'm a sneakerhead. I should have stock in NIKE by now. The slogan for Nike is "Just do It!" Its brand and name are derived from the Greek goddess Nike. Her name means victory in any field. Paul was well-versed in Greek and Roman culture. I also believe he may have been an athlete because he includes many references to track and field events. He promotes victory in this text. He states we can do all things through Christ, who gives us the strength to do them with. So know that whatever you're facing you can do it. You are strong enough to complete the task because you have been given strength from Christ. That's supernatural strength. I'm talking about Superman's strength. You can handle it, so just do it! So ask yourself this question: What's stopping me now?

List five things you will accomplish this week now that you know you can do it!

1. _____

2. _____

3. _____

4. _____

5. _____

SPREAD LOVE

2 Corinthians 6:13
As a fair exchange, I ask you as my children: Open wide your hearts also.

If you are like me you dread going to the dentist, it is never a pleasant experience. I despise it the most when I hear them say "Open Wide," which means they are about to do some work in my mouth. However, in order for them to do the work my mouth has to be wide open. They can't work in a closed mouth and God can't work in a closed heart. Paul is instructing the Corinthians to open up their hearts to God. God shows us so much love and it's only right that we reciprocate the love back to Him. One way we can show love to God is through the way we treat other people. Your task this week is to show love to others. Be nice this Week! Let the love of God pour out of you this week in everything you do. Matthew 5:16 states "Let your light so shine before men, that they may see your good works, and glorify your Father which is in heaven." Jesus wants us to be a light in the world. Light expels darkness, and love is the greatest way we can light up the world. So open wide and let the Love of God pour out of you this week and every week from this point forward. Love wins especially when it's the Love of God!

This Week's Agenda:

Think of ways you can spread love and kindness throughout your school this week!

PEACEFUL CHILDREN

Matthew 5:9
Blessed are the peacemakers, for they will be called children of God.

I consider most of my students my children and once I teach them, they belong to me forever. So as one of my kids, they need to act like they are my kids. So if they are acting up in school they are a poor representation of me because that's not how I taught them to act. The expectation is that they will put into practice the things that we have taught them, however, it is up to them how they choose to behave. We don't mind taking credit for the good things they do but we are quiet when it's something bad. What if God looks at us the same way? He has placed so much good in us and then we repay him by doing something bad. I'm sure that doesn't make him feel well. We are all his children, however, I knew at times he doesn't want to claim us! Jesus is teaching in this sermon that those who keep or make peace are called the children of God. So since we are God's kids we should be making peace instead of raising hell. God doesn't get any glory when we act a fool. So this week let's act like God's kids and make peace. Paul told the Romans to always try to make peace with all men if possible (Romans 12:18). This week it will be possible, you will make Peace. Your room or office will be the most peaceful place on Campus.

This Week's Agenda:

Titus 3:9-11
But avoid foolish controversies, genealogies, dissensions, and quarrels about the law, for they are unprofitable and worthless. As for a person who stirs up division, after warning him once and then twice, has nothing more to do with him, knowing that such a person is warped and sinful; he is self-condemned.

GREAT EXPECTATIONS

1 Peter 1:3
Praise be to the God and Father of our Lord Jesus Christ! In His great mercy, he has given us new birth into a living hope through the resurrection of Jesus Christ from the dead,

You have something to look forward to! I don't know about you but on some Monday mornings, I have to drag myself out of bed to get ready for work. Some days you may feel like you don't have anything to look forward to. I have some good news for you today, God has something great in store for you. Also because Jesus was raised from the dead, you have a living hope. The enemy thought he won when Jesus died on the cross because the "hope" of the world was dead, but that's not how the story ends. We know that he died but HE GOT UP! When Jesus got Up, we received hope. Hope here is defined as the expectation of something good. I want all of you to have an expectation of something GOOD this week. Something good is about to happen to you. Believe it and wait for it to happen. I've truly got a feeling that Everything is going to be alright for you this week. On this coming Friday, at the end of the day, you will have the revelation "This was a good week!"

This Week's Agenda:
List some Good things you expect to happen in your future.

PROMISE KEEPER

Isaiah 41:10

So do not fear, for I am with you; do not be dismayed, for I am your God.
I will strengthen you and help you; I will uphold you with my righteous right
hand.

A promise is defined as a declaration or assurance that one will do a particular thing or that a particular thing will happen. When someone makes a promise it is your hope that they keep their promise. However, in many instances, we are let down due to broken promises. There is one person that has never let me down, and that's God. I believe, receive, and stand on every promise. 2 Corinthians 1:20 teaches us that the promises of God are Yes and Amen through Jesus Christ. Therefore this helps to make the above prophecy from Isaiah so special. God gives us four promises: I am with you, I am your God, I will strengthen you and help you, and I will uphold you. Because I believe in God and His promises, this makes everything and anything that I might go through seem small. These promises assure me that everything will be alright. I believe in the promises of God. Numbers 23:19 teaches us that God does not lie so if He Said you can Believe it.

This Week's Agenda:

Your task for this week is to take God at his Word. Get in His word and find every promise God has for your life. Then I want you to get ready for your Promises to Be Fulfilled.

FOLLOW DIRECTIONS

John 15:10-11

If you keep my commands, you will remain in my love, just as I have kept my Father's commands and remain in his love. 11 I have told you this so that my joy may be in you and that your joy may be complete.

There is a reward for following instructions. Depending on the age of the students you work with, there may be some type of incentive for following your directives. The world would be a better place if everyone did as they were told, however, that will never happen. We can admit for ourselves we don't always do what we are supposed to do. Jesus reminds us here that if we follow His directions and His way, we remain in His love. In the love of Jesus is a good place to be. His love is patient and his love is kind. Jesus makes it easy for us to follow him because there is always a blessing in following Jesus. I want to keep his commandments, I want to be more like him. The reason why is that he is a great example. He is not a do as a say not as I do person. He modeled the behavior or character he wants us to follow. The New Living Translation gives this spin on v. 11, "I have told you these things so that you will be filled with my joy. Yes, your joy will overflow!" All of us should want our Joy to overflow. I need an overflow of Joy in my office, classroom, car, home, relationships, finances, family, and the list goes on. Jesus simply states that if you keep my commandments you will have an overflow of Joy. We know what we need to do, but will we do it?

This Week's Agenda:

Your task for this week is to follow the commandments of Jesus. Get in your Word and see what the Lord is telling you to do this week and JUST DO It, and watch the end result....JOY!

THE GIFT OF STRENGTH

Psalm 29:11
The Lord gives strength to his people;
the Lord blesses his people with peace.

You are almost at the end, you can and you will make it. I know you may feel like this year has drained the life out of you but I promise you that God is giving back everything that you lost. Have you ever read the account of Job's life? He lost everything just for being who God made him to be. He was attacked on every side, but he never Gave up. Because of his faithfulness, God gave him Double for his trouble. Educators, you keep the faith! God is giving you exactly what you need to finish. Strength and Peace will help you cross that finish line. We all feel the same way, "Lord just let me make it to the summer!" Guess what, God is going to give you the peace of summer before it gets here. These next two or three weeks (depending on your contract) will fly by and they will not be stressful. This scripture reminds us of two of God's character traits, he likes to give and he likes to bless. I'm excited to be on the receiving end of his giving and blessings.

This Week's Agenda:

Receive what He has for you this week, Strength and Peace, and let it carry you the rest of the week.
Make this Declaration:
"I am on the receiving end of God's Giving and Blessings!"

FAITH REWARDS

Hebrew 11:1
Now faith is confidence in what we hope for and assurance about what we do not see.

You can now see the end. At the beginning of the school year, you had faith that you could make it through to the end of the year. You had no idea what you were going to go through but through faith, you believed that you could make it. We had the confidence that we could endure to the end, and guess what we have made it to the end. We saw it by faith before it manifested in nature. We kept the faith for 36 weeks and 180 days of school. I know you wanted to give up a few of those days but you kept the faith. God rewards those who have faith. Hebrews 11:6 states "And without faith it is impossible to please God because anyone who comes to him must believe that he exists and that he rewards those who earnestly seek him." Your faith this year has pleased God. There have been many situations where you said "God I believe you can get me through it." Due to your faith in Him and your desire to be in His presence even at work, he has a reward for you. I know your paycheck doesn't reflect your work, but God has a greater reward for all of us who have endured.

This Week's Agenda:

List some of the things you have endured this year with God's help, then Praise God for Bringing you Through!

I SURVIVED

Romans 8:28
And we know that in all things God works for the good of those who love him, who[a] have been called according to his purpose.

The year has come to a close. YOU MADE IT. It's now time for you to rest and rejuvenate to prepare for the next school year. As you look back over the year, I'm sure that you have experienced a lot over these 36 weeks both good and the bad. Regardless of what you have been through, it all has worked for your Good. It has made you stronger, wiser, and better prepared for what's next. Every battle has prepared you for the next because the enemy can't surprise you anymore. After all, you have already taken his best shots and YOU SURVIVED. Every tear you have cried this year, God is about to transfer them to the flow of blessings that are coming to your life. You have been called to be an educator because it's not the money that's keeping you at that school. As you walk in your purpose remember that God is keeping and protecting you. We serve a God that loves us and in return, we love him back. There are benefits to God's love and you have reaped those benefits and the proof of that is YOU Survived the year.

This Week's Agenda:
Reflect on what worked and what didn't work. Prepare for the unexpected next year, and know that God is with you in everything that you do.